LIFE CYCLES
Sunflowers

by Robin Nelson

first step nonfiction

Lerner Publications Company · Minneapolis

This is a sunflower.

How does a sunflower grow?

3

In the spring, a sunflower
seed is planted.

Some seeds are dropped by
birds.

The sun warms the seed.

Water helps the seed
to grow.

First, a **root** comes out of the seed.

The roots get food from the
soil for the sunflower.

Then a **shoot** pushes up
through the dirt.

The shoot grows leaves on its **stem**.

The sunflower grows taller.

Next, a flower **bud** grows at the top.

One day, the flower opens.

There are seeds in the middle of the flower.

In the fall, the sunflower
will die.

But the seeds will grow new
sunflowers in the spring.

How to Grow a Sunflower

1. Find a small pot, and fill it with soil.

2. Make a hole in the soil, and drop one sunflower seed in.

3. Cover the seed with soil.

4. Put the pot in a sunny spot.

5. Keep the soil moist with water—not too dry and not too wet.

6. When your plant has at least four leaves, move it to a sunny spot outside.

Sunflower Facts

 The sunflower is one of the fastest-growing plants.

 It takes about 13 weeks for a sunflower to grow.

 Some sunflowers can grow more than 10 feet tall.

 Many people eat sunflower seeds.

 The head of a sunflower can be bigger than a dinner plate.

 Sunflower seeds are sometimes crushed to make sunflower oil. Sunflower oil is used for cooking.

 Leaves make food for the sunflower using air, rain, and the sun.

 During a day, the head of a sunflower will move to follow the sun.

Glossary

 bud – a flower that has not opened yet

 root – part of a plant that grows down into the ground

 shoot – a plant that has just started to grow

 soil – dirt or ground

 stem – part of a plant that grows above the ground

Index

The photographs in this book are reproduced through the courtesy of: © iStockphoto.com/Lisa Kyle Young, p. 2; © iStockphoto.com/appletat, p. 3; © Karlene Schwartz, pp. 4, 6; © WILLIAM OSBORN/naturepl.com, p. 5; © Niclas Albinsson/Jupiterimages, p. 7; © Dwight Kuhn , pp. 8, 10, 22 (second and third from top); © Todd Strand/Independent Picture Service, pp. 9, 22 (second from bottom); © Nigel Cattlin/Visuals Unlimited/Getty Images, p. 11; © Julie Caruso, p. 12; © Julie Caruso/Independent Picture Service, pp. 13, 14, 15, 16, 22 (top); © iStockphoto.com/Tomas Bercic, p. 17; © Nigel Cattlin/Visuals Unlimited/Getty Images, p. 22 (bottom), illustrations by © Laura Westlund/Independent Picture Service.

Front cover; © Royalty-Free/CORBIS.

Lerner Publications Company
A division of Lerner Publishing Group, Inc.
241 First Avenue North
Minneapolis, MN 55401 U.S.A.

Website address: www.lernerbooks.com

Library of Congress Cataloging-in-Publication Data

Nelson, Robin, 1971–
     Sunflowers / by Robin Nelson.
         p.   cm. — (First step nonfiction. Plant life cycles)
     Includes index.
     ISBN: 978–0–7613–4072–0 (lib. bdg. : alk. paper)
     1. Sunflowers—Life cycles—Juvenile literature. I. Title. II. Series.
QK495.C74.N45 2009
635.9'3399—dc22   2008033747

Manufactured in the United States of America
1 2 3 4 5 6 – DP – 14 13 12 11 10 09